POETIC HEART

A Restorative Journey

by Janet Edwards

Conscious Dreams
PUBLISHING

Poetic Heart: A Restorative Journey

First Printed in United Kingdom 2023

Published by Conscious Dreams Publishing
www.consciousdreamspublishing.com

Edited by Elise Abram and Daniella Blechner

Typeset by Oksana Kosovan

ISBN: 978-1-915522-39-9

DEDICATION

This book of gems is dedicated to my earthly dads Cecil Smart and Malcom Edwards who have transitioned from earth and left deep and beautiful imprints on my heart.

Thanks for birthing me into this world Mum, love you.

It is also dedicated to my two favourite people. Thanks for your continued support and encouragement with this project and life in general. I love you both dearly, Janine Edwards and Michelle Smart. You are both such lovely souls: kind, humble and generous. Janine you are talented beyond words looking forward to your EP; it's going to be epic and Michelle you're super intelligent and your attention to detail is amazing (manuals, really)!

CONTENTS

HEARTBREAK

HURT HEARTS

So confusing
Living in deception
I tried to walk away so many times
I didn't have the fortitude, the power of abuse
I held on to those lies, denying my truth
I wanted her life to be different
Then eventually came that day
After all of the emotional and financial abuse
The unkind words, your stories, the lies
Metaphorically, you reached your hand into my chest
Pulled out my beating heart
Watched it gasping for air in your hand
As you gazed at me, uncaring
You then preceded to drop said heart to the ground
And as though that pain was not enough
You proceeded to stamp on it
Continuing to grind it into the ground
The ramifications huge
Denial, broken relationships
Too many for this opening page.

HE DID IT

In the midst of such excruciating pain
In came my Creator
When I called out His name, *Jehovah*
Deliver and vindicate me
He took me in His arms, held me closely
The process began, my squashed and bleeding heart
Put back together again
It wasn't always easy, truth be told, it was mostly hard
Self-discovery, picking up esteem
The road to wholeness often rocky
Leaving behind comfort zones, that gave no comfort
Now let me take you on this journey of inner healing.

MILLION PIECES

Watching you struggle to breathe
Almost took my breath from me
Saying goodbye eternally
One can never imagine
Then came your final breath, hands raised
That pain sits with me, my heart broken into a million
pieces
Over time each day another piece being restored
It's been a while now, and
My journey to wholeness after you continues Dad
Your humour and laughter missed for ever.

PIECES

My heart was once broken in a million pieces
How would I recover?
The question it seemed remained unanswered
My heart so fragile and left in turmoil
How do I bring the pieces back together?
Where do I start to mend this broken heart?
Bit by bit You have shown me the road to recovery
You've taught me how to let go
Even of myself and my intricacies
Your healing power delivers me
I recognise that love still flows
And You can hold a million pieces.

DADDY — YOU LEFT

It's been a while since You left me
I never realised how much I would miss you, not seeing
your face
Although I see you in me
I miss resting on your shoulder
When life got hard and I sought comfort
Not hearing your voice is painful
Never hearing your laughter excruciating
I still feel like you were taken too quickly
Yet again you have left me, now physically
Previously, emotionally
We never had that chance to really connect
Extenuating circumstances
My father but for years distant
But sitting here thinking about you
My heart aches endlessly
Tears come easily; you told me you'd miss me
I didn't want to hear it and dismissed it quickly
All I can say now, is I miss you too Daddy.

AUTO PILOT

Listening not learning
Touching not feeling
Feeling so, so empty
Smiling—heart is empty
Life flying by in slow motion
I could not have comprehended
This pain I feel when Your life ended
Talking, not making sense
Looking, seeing nothing
Nothing that I want to see
It's not a dream
This is my reality
Heart so heavy
Feels like you've left me all over again.

DECEPTIVE LOVE

Deceitful in nature
Deceptive in frame
Unkind at best
Conceited at worst
Your heart unloving and unkind
It does not contain truth
It does, however, contain yourself
You are more important
Than those around you, your belief
It does not matter who it hurts
So long as it's not you, truth?
You think you're king of my castle
That's not true
My heart is protected by God
Against characters like you
I no longer believe your truth
Your heart and your actions, not true
I realise that the only person you love is you.

SPACED LOVE

There are times that it seems that love hurts
This makes no logical sense
As love in itself does not bring harm
But this is a different kind of love
When scrutinised closer it's actually not love at all
It's a form of control, pretending to be what it can't be
Hurting others, because it's hurting itself
A complicated notion, but reality for many
The way that you treat me
Tells me how you feel about yourself, for this I'm sorry
I'm having to learn not to judge, based on how you make me feel
Easier said than done because I instinctively want treat you the same
This is when loving from a distance helps
Though not my ideal and I hope will change
But loving from a distance helps me with boundaries
As its anxiety inducing being around you
Strange, maybe but that's the best I can say to explain
My love has grown towards you, for now I just need space.

GOD'S LOVE

STRENGTH OF HEART

Your strength, my heart
Strengthen my heart when it wants to fade
Help me to know in Your hands it's safe
Establish laughter in my life again
When my heart wants to tell me, this is the end
Give me the tenacity to overcome pain
To allow Your love in my heart again
To never lose hope because the road appears rocky
To retreat behind defence mechanisms
Or allow my foundation to become shaky
You are the King of my heart
Help me Lord to do my part.

CREATOR IS LOVE

Who hung the moon in place?
Who causes the sun to shine
Then causes it to set again?
Who sprinkled the stars into the heavens
And clouds that move so gracefully?
Who puts a song in my heart in the midnight hour?
Who can breathe on a dead soul and cause it to live again?
Who can take less than nothing
And make it into something?
Who placed a dream in my heart
Then causes it to come to pass?
Who can do exceedingly and abundantly above all I ask
or think?
Who but the Sovereign King the Prince of Peace
He is Jehovah the creator of everything.

*Genesis 1:1 In the beginning God created the heavens and
the earth.*

HEART BE STILL

Be comforted, oh heart be still
Worry is all too easy, just trust Him
Height can't be added, nor number of days
The quietened heart can sing His praise
Look beyond the darkness
Reach beyond pain
Take courage my heart, love and be still
And know Jehovah is your God.

TURMOIL

Heart in turmoil
Which way to turn
Trying to run
Escaping the pain
Seasons at a time
This is relentless
Then my spirit
Gives my heart a message
You may seem heavy
Come to me, you will find safely
Bleeding hearts my speciality
Stop trying to live in uncertainty
Crying heart, drowning serenity
I will give you peace
Give your tumultuous heart to me
I will give you security.

HEART TRANSFIXED

My question to you is this
How do you heal what cannot be fixed?
My heart so guarded, I told myself it's normal
Normal to keep people at arm's length
My reality however, told me something different
People at arm's length denied me of intimacy and
friendships
How do I love You, let You in, when in the past all I have
known is pain?
You are so kind so gracious; You show me where I went
wrong
Trying to love, but denying me, clearly this is fantasy
Love others as you love yourself, now I know why this
didn't sit well
The love for myself tainted
Looking at me with judgements, so many judgments
You have made: 'Why can't you? You are not worthy
Now comes another story, You have loved me regardless
I have learnt to love me too, even those dark places
Yes, I have done things I am not proud of
Things I am ashamed of
I accept I cannot change the past, but I can live in the
moment
I can get excited about the future

As my heart picks up pace and begins to live and beat again
I breathe a sigh of relief, You really never left me or
relinquished Your love for me
I am so grateful, I get to understand You as my Father
An incredible journey of self-discovery and life
achievements
Truly You have been my footprints in the sand.
Lovingly You have held my hand
Even in the times I hid from You and refused to talk,
patiently You waited
When I saw the ugliness of my heart, You helped me to not
fall apart
You restored me, graciously, lovingly You held my heart
Again, I feel set apart, what else can I say
You have transfixed my heart.

PURE GRACE

Love never-ending and pure
Love that has kept me this far
Even when disappointed
Your love — Your love prevails
Deeper than the deepest seas
Higher that the outer spheres
Beyond the stars, moon and time itself
Totally unconditional, who compares
Your loving kindness holds me still
My heart knows all too well, that love can be futile
It often ends before it begins
Love unchanging, pure and true
Straight from the throne room
You hold me true.

GREAT LOVE

I've searched high, I've searched low
I thought I found it in him, then in them
It was almost tangible then seemed to escape
It crept up behind me, metaphorically slapped me
in the face
Then I realised it wasn't real, it wasn't authentic anyways
Not the way I expected it to be
Too much pressure on another
How could I expect them to make me happy?
Love I now realise comes from within
And it's a two-way street
How could I have missed it?
It was there in plain sight
Waiting for me to discover and embrace its reality
I realise the greatest Love we can have here on earth
comes from within
When you find it, you realise it's Him, the Creator
He will teach you to love yourself before you try to love
another.

*John 5:13 Greater love has no one than this: to lay down
one's life for one's friends.*

FOREVER PRESENT

I wake up You're there
I go through the day You're there
You hear the silence of my heart speaking
I say nothing — yet You understand me
Even when I go about my everyday life, busy, busy, busy
When I sit down quietly You are ready to listen to me
You never impose Yourself on me
I don't even understand why You bother about me
How You love me goes beyond my human comprehension
Unconditional is what they say
You have proved this to be true time and time again
When I am not sure which way to go
Or get to the point I want to do a round about turn
Your still voice beckons me to stay
I will never leave or forsake you — You say
You are awesome Father, You energise me
There is nothing that can separate me
When life knocks me down
And it does knock me down from time to time
That left hook came from nowhere
Even then You reach down for me
And remind me 'knocked down'
But you my child never knocked out.
2 Cor 4:9 Persecuted, but not forsaken; cast down,
but not destroyed;

HEART WANTS

The heart wants what the heart wants
But is it what it needs?
Broken love a human disease
Betrayal second nature to some
How to trust in a world fallen
Heart confused, heavy-laden
Believing truth for lies
And lies as fundamental truth
You must give to get
But You challenge that trend
The heart wants what it wants
Take a moment, what does it need
The love of a Saviour, so pure so true
Unconditional, inherently purposeful
My heart wants what it wants and that's YOU.

TRUTHFUL HEART

Heart be true
Your Heavenly Father does love you
Words going back and forth
Not trusting, not faithful, they don't ring true
You've abandoned me
My heart in conflict with my words
My heart may have been broken
But they that wait on Him will never be ashamed
Faithfulness, one of Your characteristics
My heart wants to deny, it just can't
For You have never left me
Even from my broken place
Truth, Your truth rings true within me.

INSATIABLE

Insatiable in its desire for freedom
The words unloved despicable in nature
Irresistible are the words from Your throne
More than aspirational, Your word brings calm
The propensity to walk with You
Confuses my heart's stubborn voice
To push You away and hide in my own day
The inclination to believe the lie
Proclivity at its finest hour
Yet Your voice conspicuous, soothing brings clarity
I say I can't, You know I can
My heart sleeps and slumbers under the weight of its
betrayal
Vociferous Your Word surrounds me
Rambunctious they take their place
Peace and safety where I now dwell
Freedom, my heart in Your ever-increasing loving well.

FORGIVING HEART

There was a time my heart was so broken
So badly, I'm sure it was bleeding
Shattered into tiny pieces
My question was, how am I going to forgive?
You lovingly told me, You will give me the strength
You took me to scriptures that were so hard to read
Pray for those who wilfully use you
Surely, You've got to be joking
But as hard as it was
Your word brought me such peace
You had the patience to take me through the process
And the day that I prayed, what sweet relief
My understanding struggled to take in that peace
You simply amazed me
You are totally outstanding
There is no one else like You and never will be
Who are You? My Comforter, my Peace, my Teacher,
my Friend
Who are You? The one who escorts me into the
presence of God
Both in this world and the next
You are Irreplaceable, Irresistible, absolutely
Incredible
You are the Holy Spirit — You are God.

UNKNOWN LANGUAGE

My heart began to speak a language I didn't understand
I had doubts, not only about Your face but also Your hand
Are You really guiding me?
And if so, why so much pain?
Only to be reminded every loss has a gain
You reminded me Your plans for me are good
Even with a saddened heart
You reminded me I have a future and a special hope.

YOU'VE ALWAYS LOVED ME

You didn't stop speaking, I stopped listening
For this I'm so sorry,
I'm sorry I disconnected from my true source
Disappointment came and lied to me
And I believed wholeheartedly
I believed that perhaps You didn't love me
Perhaps You had not forgiven me
Areas of guilt and shame consumed me, instead of
believing what You had told me
You said You'd never leave or forsake me
You know everything about me, my poor decisions and
bad habits
Yet You still love me, today I declare that I love You too
Daddy God, Abba Father, I'm so sorry, forgive me and
I thank You for forgiving me
I accept You and Your Love
Gratitude my feeling towards You
Your faithfulness surrounds and reminds me of Your
kindness
Yes, Your love is faithful and unconditional
I just need to fully believe it,
I ask myself how could this be?
How can You love the likes of me?
Then I'm beautifully reminded that Your thoughts are
not my thoughts

Neither are Your ways my ways, You love me because You
can and do
And because that's who You are, the great 'I Am'
I'm so grateful You love me, even when I struggle to
My heart will sing and praise You for all eternity.

RESTORATION

GRATEFUL HEART

It's been a while since my heart felt
To block all pain, it's been fortified with self
But is lonely here and grief seems ever present
Self has not helped me on this journey
In fact, I have been greatly hindered
So, as I relinquish self and trust in You again
My heart is grateful for all You have done
My heart is grateful for what You continue to do
My heart is grateful for bringing me back to You.

HEART BE STILL

Heart dancing to an external tune
Rhythmic Creator secondary now
Anxiety, self-pity have me dancing their tune
But that's not who I am
Confusion, disappointment taking my attention
Heart keeps fighting beyond apprehension
From beyond the veil, a sound of comfort
A small still voice, whispers oh so gently
Heart be still
I am with you, always have been and will always be
Forgiving, accepting, you're my masterpiece
Heart now put aside false imagination
Heart now be still and trust Me again.

HEART OF HOPE

So many dark days and unsettled nights
Heart wondering which way to go
Holding on to questions passed
Answers in my stony heart take a moment, reflect, review
Has He ever left you?
It has certainly felt that way on occasion
Everything challenged, including my faith
As I reflect deeper still
I recognise my hope is in You
The more my heart is buffed and challenged
I am reassured my hope is in You
For You know the end from beginning
My life is predestined for greatness, I believe it
My heart come let's hope again.

JUST WHEN

Darkness so dark in its nature
Seems relentless and unforgiving
Whirls and dances in my heart
Goes beyond, subdues my soul
Downcast, sad days, long nights
How do I break free from this agonising hell?
Can I ever be set free again?
Has this become my reality, is this the end?
A shimmer of hope comes through
Heart be still, light no matter how small, penetrates
darkness every time
It can't hide, although it tries
Darkness cowers at Light's voice
I look up from my downward stance
Just when I thought life was over
Light came gallantly through
Reminding me of all the things You can do
Be strong in Me, I'll take Your weakness
Your tears, I understand that language
As always You are right on time
Just when I think I can't, You remind me I can.

YOUR HEART

I never considered how this may have affected you
I didn't think of the trauma caused and who you had to tell
It didn't occur to me what you went through
Tongues wagging, judging, condemning, a sense of shame
From my perspective at times it was grim
But my heart didn't allow me to consider him
All consumed by what laid ahead
Carrying evidence of what happened in bed
Now finally I can acknowledge your stress
And can truly say I wish you God's best.

OPEN

Be Brave, open for business again
Love lost and love hurt
Does not hold the foundations for my future
Barricades and whimsical smiles
A façade, or are they, dancing on my parade
Open up let it in
Your old, your new friend called Love
Let's do this thing again…

LOVE AGAIN

Controversy rides the waves of my heart
Can I or should I trust again?
A heartbroken many times
Broken in so many different ways
Yet the waves subside to Your voice
I have loved you with an everlasting love
I've never left, is His response
Controversy retreats, taken its flight
It may be hard at times
But Your love never wains
And yes, my heart can and will love again.

ANOTHER CHANCE

So, you feel you can't love again
Or is it that you don't want to love again
Reluctant to walk this path of vulnerabilities
Wanting nothing more than to protect my heart
Scared of the question to be asked
Can I love completely?
I know You do me
But recovering from betrayal is easier said than done
Vulnerabilities path requires action
Letting go and trusting again
Can I love again?
In You, I believe I can and will love again.

EXPECTANT HEART

Expectant and apprehensive
Excited yet unsure
Can my heart really embrace this new season?
Can my heart truly love again?
Is it true that You've always loved me?
I ask the question, but I know the truth
You are always there even when I'm hurting
My pain is no indicator of Your loving-kindness
It does not reflect You, Your essence is love
You present Yourself to help me live beyond pain
By Your gracious love, I breathe again.

SMILE AGAIN

Smile again just for this moment

Even if it feels too temporal

Your heart will thank you

Why be burdened with things you can't change

Smile at your storm, take courage my heart

You may be hurting in this moment

But moments come and they go

Give peace to your heart

By not perpetually wondering about the future, or visiting
the past

Heart, smile now and give yourself the gift of gratitude.

DESERVING OF LOVE

I believed the lie
Undeserving of love
Refusing, even rejected Your heart towards me
Feeling I was unworthy
The sad life I lived, worthy of me
Not appreciating this is not my destiny
Even though my heart feels empty
My heart has become accepting
'Not so,' I hear You say
'My love towards you never changed
As far as the East is from the West
So, My love is never ending
Hear Me when I say
Your heart is very safe in My love
And always has been.'

Deuteronomy 31:8 It is the LORD who goes before you. He will be with you; he will not leave you or forsake you.

UNKIND

You love me you say
Your actions are unnerving
Very contradicting
Actions, they say, speak louder than words
My heart is not getting what it deserves
Empty promises and unkind words
My heart, my love is in reserve
Travelling at high velocity towards empty
My heart is in meltdown
Trying to make sense of confusion
How do you love me?
You don't respect me?
Is my life is not your dumping ground?
Not so, I deserve better and you've hindered my growth
Clearly, you are not a part of my life's journey.

MY LOVE

Believe the lie, not I
Rejecting your negativity
The feeling of being underserving
Foreign territory
And does not sit well with me
Not my destiny
Hiding from love is exasperating
My heart knows, it's exhausting
You have me in a corner
Trying to whisper lies to me
But I know I am worthy of Love
Grateful my love has finally found me.

GRATEFUL

Happy for daylight
Thrilled to see rainbows in the sky
Excited about new prospects
Encouraged when all is well
Ecstatic when I hear my child's laughter
Delighted by my favourite people
Proud of their achievements
Exhilarated by fresh air
Euphoric when my heart is still
Jubilant, even in my insecurities
Only because I know You hold me
Grateful my heart can always be still in You.

FORTRESS

My heart a fortress
Protecting its borders
It's been deceived before
My quest no more
In doing so, have I missed a faithful suitor?
The stakes are high
My walls are higher
Substitute on the side lines
Willing me to be braver
Commitment a hard place
Loneliness, unthinkable, undeniable
Fortress you need to fall
Heart be prepared to give
And receive His all.

MYSTERIOUS

The human heart, a mystery
Without love it's a misery
Love gives, Love comes to me
Yet still I run, undeserving, not so
The thought of not having You
Leaves me oh so empty
The thought of loving You
Brings me plenty
Peace, joy, contentment
Loving nature, truth, its reality
Sentimental my thoughts
From You genuine, unyielding
Come intertwine, this heart of mystery
Let's walk in destiny
You and me.

EXPECTANT HEART

Expectant not anxious
Magnificent and brilliant
True beyond truth
Veracity and Genuine
Authentic and legitimate
Faithful and kind
Caring and comforting
Understanding and unchanging
Compassionate and loving
Benevolent and generous
My heart yearns for You.

CHANGED HEART

My heart will praise You
Even when I look back at the hurts
You know my steps, the steps I would take
Joy in my suffering, oh so hard, not always achieved
As I think about it, I tried to disregard
I just wanted to forget the past
I couldn't understand, my question, WHY?
Count it all joy, You say
Help me Father to obey
And not to disregard or conceal pain
Help me to learn, encourage others
As pain no longer dwells in my heart
I stand in Your presence
My garments have changed
My heart a soiree as I give You praise.

AGAIN

My heart will love again
Light will shine from the broken places
Strengthened by Your purity
Transparency in all its glory
My heart will hold Yours
In a place of safety
I am willing to be open
Allowing Your love to come in
To commune and guide me
My heart loves again
Your heart and mine, eternal friends.

WHEN

When I think You've done all You can
You do that little bit more
When I feel I just can't go on
You open that door
When I turn and walk away
You reach Your hands towards me
When I say I no longer love You
You are still right there beside me
When I think it's the end, it's over
You remind me You'll never leave or forsake me
When the pain seems too much to bear
You take the wings of the morning visit and heal me
You keep me and restore me
When I think You've done all You can
Lord Jesus You always do much more.

HAPPY WITH ME

Can it be, somebody loves me
Enjoys my company
Accepts me as I am
Not trying to change me
They see my inner beauty
Encouraging me to be a better version of me
You've invited me in
Into places you had hidden previously
I understand abandonment issues, as do you
Walls had gone up and defences took their place
Yet despite our apparent issues
My heart breathes when I see you
The sound of your voice makes me smile
You have confided in me your deepest fears
I have done the same
Both dubious about loving again
But there's that something about you, a purity within
Despite the impression, you may think I believe
Yes, we've been found, there is a love unashamed
You've invited me in, your invitation I have gracefully
received
Time to let love grow, and show forth His glory.

LETTING GO

For so long I held on to that pain
Questioning your integrity
Thought of you with distain
I held my pain so proudly
Not taking responsibility for how I was feeling
Your fault was all I wanted to know and say
I did not take the time to look within
I was careless with my heart strings
But then I craved healing
This journey was exhausting
My heart fortified like a regal mansion
Protecting its prowess and its pride
I was not getting out and no one was coming in
Pride before a fall was becoming my reality
Relationships falling all around me
When all I wanted was to love and be loved
Tainted and traumatised by past events
My only hope was letting go
Letting go of my bitterness, letting go of my pride
Letting go of the pain in order to love again.

*Isaiah 43:19 Look, I am about to do something new; even
now it is coming. Do you not see it? Indeed, I will make
a way in the wilderness, rivers in the desert.*

SO, YOU THINK

It's over, you can't love again
There is no way you want to experience that pain
The pain of a loved one walking away
Although it's also painful if they stay
Esteem on the ground, gaslighting all around
Red is blue and black is white
Flags flying on different levels, all ignored
Maya Angelou once said, 'When someone shows you who
they are believe them.'
Words can be so cheap and deceiving
Our heart often informs us, but we don't believe instead, we
cling to the lies
Holding on to fantasy that flies in our skies
Our heart tells us we are unhappy
Societal norms tell us this is it, it's okay
Let me tell you it's possible to love again
Firstly, start with you, love from within
I know it can be hard but it's a good place to begin
Each day take a moment to appreciate; no need to wait
Be thankful for this a brand-new day
It may feel hard right now but it's not impossible
Your heart can love again.

NAKED LOVE

Unpretentious
Comes with no stories
No 'you give me, and I'll see what I can do'
It's caring and kind
Characteristics that can be hard to find
But once found blows my mind
Natural, you help me to be me
Not demeaning, to make you feel better
Able to challenge unhealthy views lovingly
I support you to be you and grow
Not judging you based on the last unsavoury character
The last deception that still had my attention
This love is not showy
There's no need to be grand
Your love tells me you will always hold my hand
Naked love in its purest form
Comes from above
It's not abusive or controlling
You are the epitome of a God enlightened man
This love embraces and brings positive change
It's a unique kind of love
It makes me feel safe
It's Your perfect love, that flows through him to me
And me to Him.

PERMISSION PLEASE

Permission to love me unequivocally
To love me, the way You do
Unconditional, warts and all
You see past my shortcomings
You look straight into my heart
I, on the other hand seem to take pleasure in pulling myself
apart
When all the time You are ready with that new start
Ready to give me that pure clean heart
Permission to love me the way You do
Then I can reach out and love others in purity too
Permission to see through Your eyes
That voice from within
My child permission has always been granted
Permission was never needed
You just need to understand who you are
Made in my image, stand on My Word
Born to have dominion and walk in my joy
You ask Me, 'how can I love you'?
I created You; I formed you in your mother's womb
You're my masterpiece, carried in my heart, and always
have been.

FALSE PROTECTION

Protected or so I thought
Until I realised the thing I craved most, had been locked out
You see, I needed to protect my heart
So, I fortified it with thoughts of '*I don't care*'
Withdrew slowly, subtly so no one noticed
Conversations became surface
Trapped in my own world of superficial smiles
Decided never to let someone mistreat my heart again
It was left disconnected and trampled, never again
What I didn't realise I was nursing a hardened heart
It happened over time, it became unresponsive
This became my new normal, distrust and cynical views
Unwilling to let love in, for the fear of being hurt again
Then one day in my isolated space, where friends became
scarce
I recognised an uncomfortable truth, by fortifying my heart,
I had locked love out
My prayer then became, '*Soften my heart Lord, make it flesh
again*'
As it softened and became more vulnerable
There was a peace and safety in knowing that You said, You
will never leave me
I'm grateful to You as love found its way back home
Resting in a heart that You created
Loving again is such a privilege, my heart once again, flesh.

LOVE RESTORED

It's been a while
Irregular beating
I trust You, then I don't
I forgive, then I can't, it hurts
Grace captures and I forgive again
You loved into that empty place
I'm filled with love again
My broken heart restored and healed.

SUPREME LOVE — AWESOME GOD

Your ways are not my ways
Neither are Your thoughts
You were not afraid of my tantrums
Or my disruptive heart
Instead, You reached out to me in love
You told me it's okay and that you have a plan
You remind me that I am in the palm of your hand
You healed me thoroughly, as only You can
When I called out to You, I was not shunned
Thank you, Awesome Father, for yet another chance
Thank you for loving me despite the things I have done
Reminding me, I'm loved the way I am
Now my heart's desire is Jehovah
Let Your will be done…
I let go of past indiscretions
Those received and those done
My desire, to walk with You, thank you for holding my hand.

Isaiah 41:13 For I am the Lord your God who takes hold of your right hand and says to you, do not fear; I will help you.

Conscious Dreams
PUBLISHING

Transforming diverse writers
into successful published authors

www.consciousdreamspublishing.com

authors@consciousdreamspublishing.com

Let's connect

Ingram Content Group UK Ltd.
Milton Keynes UK
UKHW020643260723
425809UK00016B/654